Traditions Around The World

Food

by Jillian Powell

Thomson Learning
New York

Traditions Around The World

Body Decoration

Costumes

Dance

Food

Games

Jewelry

Masks

Musical Instruments

Consultant: Anthony Shelton, Keeper of Non-Western Art and Anthropology, Royal Pavilion Art Gallery and Museums, Brighton, England.

First published in the United States in 1995 by Thomson Learning New York, NY

Published simultaneously in Great Britain in 1995 by Wayland (Publishers) Ltd.

U.K. version copyright © 1995 Wayland (Publishers) Ltd.

U.S. version copyright © 1995 Thomson Learning

Library of Congress Cataloging-in-Publication Data
Powell, Jillian.
　Food / by Jillian Powell.
　　p.　cm.—(Traditions around the world)
　Includes bibliographical references (p.　) and index.
　ISBN 1-56847-346-X
　1.Food habits—Juvenile Literature. [1. Food habits.]
　I. Title. II. Series.
GT2860.P69　　1995
394.1'2—dc20　　　　　　　　94-46639

Printed in Italy

COVER: A Fulani woman in Kanem, Chad, making butter in a traditional way.

Picture acknowledgments:
The publishers wish to thank the following for providing the photographs for this book:
Cephas Picture Library, 3 (top, right Sand Hambrook, left Graham Wicks), 16 (Eric Burt), 37 (Nigel Blythe); Bruce Coleman Ltd 16-17 (Dr. Eckart Pott), 20 (Charles Henneghien), 22 (Brian Henderson), 28-9 (Frans Lanting), 33 (Brian Henderson); Eye Ubiquitous 6 (Grenville Turner), 23 (inset, John Miles), 24 (John Miles), 25 (top, Mike Atkins), 32-3 (James Davis), 35 (top, Frank Leather, bottom, Simon Arnold), 36 (Bennett Dean), 43 (Grenville Turner), 44 (Matthew McKee); Jim Holmes 8-9, 12; Life File 40 (Flora Torrance); PHOTRI 25 (bottom, Ellsworth), 28 (Bachmann), 39 (Nowitz); South American Pictures 21(Robert Francis); Tony Stone Worldwide) COVER (Jacques Jangoux), 10 (Martin Koretz), 23 (main, Robert Frerck), 30 (bottom, John Garrett), 31 (Ian Murphy), 42, 45 (David Hiser), ; Topham Picture Source 10-11, 13 (both), 14, 19, 40-41; Wayland Picture Library 6-7, 9, 15, 18, 32, 34; Laura Zito 38.
Artwork by Peter Bull.

Contents

Food around the world

▲ A Huichol woman in Mexico hanging corn out to dry.

A woman selling ▶ cassava, a traditional and widespread African food.

4

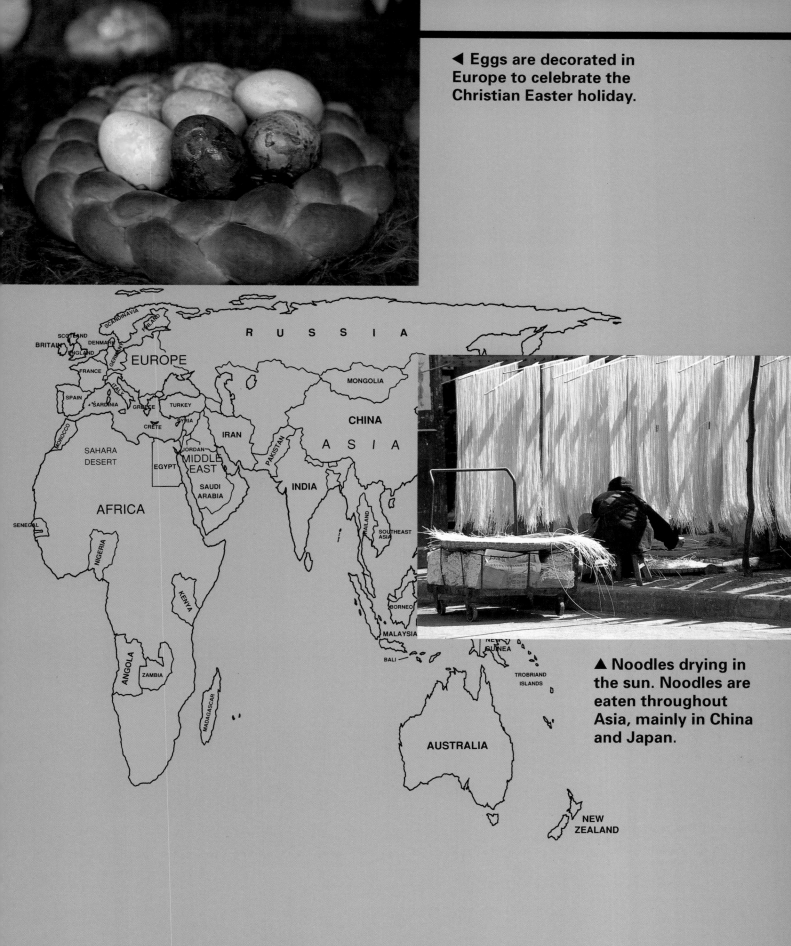

◄ Eggs are decorated in Europe to celebrate the Christian Easter holiday.

▲ Noodles drying in the sun. Noodles are eaten throughout Asia, mainly in China and Japan.

Introduction

There are many ancient traditions surrounding the preparation, cooking, and eating of food around the world. These have been shaped by the geography and climates of various countries and by the cultures, religions, and lifestyles of their peoples. The staple crops grown in a region often give rise to traditional recipes, cooking methods, and planting or harvest rituals. Foods that are especially important to a culture may carry religious or symbolic meaning and may be part of that culture's beliefs. In Mexico, South America, and parts of Africa, for example, where corn is the staple crop, there are many traditional dishes containing corn, and every year there are ceremonies connected with the planting and harvesting of it. In China and Japan, Southeast Asia, and parts of India, rice is the staple crop and is eaten with every meal. Festivals are held to celebrate the rice harvest, and some cultures even worship rice spirits.

Aboriginal peoples ▶ are traditionally hunter gatherers, taking their food from the natural environment.

6

◄ In many parts of the world, it is traditional to eat sitting around a cloth on the floor. This family in southern India is eating food served on banana leaves.

Religion and culture are both important influences on food traditions. Some religions lay down strict rules regarding foods that may or may not be eaten and the ways in which food should be prepared. Muslims must obey the food laws of their holy book, the Koran. Jews follow the rules set down in their holy scriptures. Neither Muslims nor Jews eat pork because they believe the pig is an unclean animal, while people who follow the Hindu faith eat no beef, because the cow is a sacred animal in their religion and culture.

In some religions food is a traditional offering to the gods, to give thanks for a good harvest or to prevent the anger of the gods. Food may also commemorate a special time or event. In the ancient Shinto religion of Japan, priests take traditional breakfast offerings of fish, fruit, rice, and vegetables to shrines to give thanks to the god of nature. For some religious ceremonies, foods such as fruit and vegetables are elaborately arranged, and specially prepared sweet dishes may be offered at altars or in front of statues. In Malaysia, sweet foods garnished with leaves, grasses, or flowers are offered to the Hindu god Ganesa at festival time, and coconuts are smashed in front of his statue.

7

Many food traditions are connected with religious festivals or other celebrations. Hot-cross buns, traditionally eaten during the time leading up to Easter, remind Christians of Christ's crucifixion. Matzoh, or unleavened bread, eaten by Jews during Passover, reminds them of the time the Israelites escaped from slavery in Egypt, leaving in such a hurry that they had no time to wait for their baking bread to rise.

Different cultures all over the world celebrate important times such as New Year with special feasts. Some cultures traditionally eat sweet foods, such as the honey cake eaten in Russia to bring a sweet New Year. Others eat foods believed to bring good luck; in Japan, New Year foods are in the lucky colors of red and white.

Some food traditions relate to the history or mythology of a culture. American Thanksgiving is a feast that commemorates the first successful harvest of the pilgrims who settled in Plymouth, Massachusetts in 1620. The Chinese Moon Festival, which is held at the time of the full moon in the fall, celebrates an ancient Chinese legend. People make colorful lanterns, carry burning incense sticks to greet the moon, and feast on moon-shaped pastries and fruits.

Food is also an important part of celebrations for birthdays, coming-of-age, initiation rites, and marriage and death customs. In many countries, it is traditional to bake a special cake to celebrate a birthday or a marriage. In Africa, young Masai men celebrate reaching manhood by drinking blood from a bullock and feasting on meat and milk. Cattle are so important to the lifestyle and beliefs of the Masai that bullocks are killed only for important ceremonies like this.

Often, foods traditionally eaten or offered at celebrations carry symbolic meaning. Throwing rice at weddings in India, Japan, and other countries and

serving eggs at wedding feasts in Malaysia are both believed to bring babies for a newly married couple.

Like our homes, clothes, and other belongings, the foods we eat can show our wealth and status in society. Some foods are traditionally associated with the rich and others with the poor. Staple foods such as bread, corn, potatoes, and beans often provide the basic diet of the poor. Food that is hard to obtain or to produce can be a sign of wealth and status. Asparagus, for example, which was described over 2,000 years ago by the Roman writer Pliny as a food for the rich, remains an expensive, highly prized food. Chocolate, which was once drunk by Aztec rulers, is still a luxury and is often given as a gift.

Different cultures have different customs in the way food is prepared, cooked, served, and eaten. Asian people often eat from a low table or from a cloth spread on the floor. In Africa, it is traditional for people to sit in a circle on the floor and use their fingers to help themselves from a large shared dish. In some areas, such as Southeast Asia, food is served on banana leaves. Many African and Asian peoples traditionally eat with the right hand. Chopsticks are used for eating in China and Japan, while in some countries a spoon and fork or knife and fork are used.

◀ Some foods are highly decorative, like these *lebkuchen*, or gingerbreads, made in Germany.

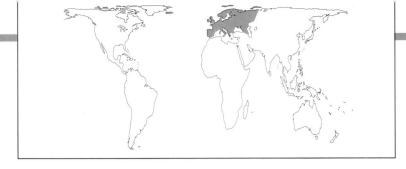

Europe

In Europe, the forty days before the Christian Easter holiday, known as Lent, were once a time for fasting. No fat, butter, or eggs could be eaten during Lent, so these foods would be used up in a pancake feast the day before Lent began. Nowadays, some Christians avoid certain foods during Lent to remind them of Christ's fasting in the wilderness, and Pancake Day is still widely celebrated in Europe. This day is also known as Mardi Gras, or Fat Tuesday. The Russian pancake feast, *Maslenitsa*, lasts for a whole week. Blini (Russian pancakes) are served with hot butter or smetana, a kind of sour cream.

Foods traditionally eaten at Easter are symbolic of the new life following Christ's resurrection and the coming of spring. At Easter, people give each other eggs, a tradition that can be traced back to ancient China and Mesopotamia. Today, it is usual to give chocolate Easter eggs. In France, Germany, and Italy, children hunt for eggs hidden in the house or garden. In Russia, hard-boiled eggs are brightly painted or dyed and exchanged as Easter gifts. At Easter, Russians enjoy eating a special soft cheese, called paskha, and bake tall, saffron-scented cakes. In many countries, hot-cross buns are traditionally eaten during Lent. These spiced buns have been eaten since the Middle Ages. The spices remind people of the spices used to prepare Christ's body for the tomb, and the cross pattern represents his crucifixion.

Mincemeat pies have been baked for Christmas since medieval times. ▶

▲ Traditional foods, such as this paskha cheese and this Kulich cake from Russia, are eaten in many European countries at Easter.

Mincemeat pies are another medieval tradition at Christmas. These were originally called crib pies because they were made in the shape of a crib with a pastry baby Jesus on top. They were once filled with ground meat, but nowadays the filling is usually made of raisins and other dried fruits. In Britain, turkeys used to be eaten only at Christmas. In eighteenth-century England, turkeys were marched, wearing special boots, from Norfolk to London in time for Christmas! Rich fruit puddings and cakes are also traditional Christmas foods.

In France, a special cake called a *gâteau des rois* is baked for Twelfth Night. Traditionally, a bean is hidden inside, although nowadays a little plastic star or moon is often used, and whoever finds the lucky bean is king or queen for the day. In Denmark, the Twelfth Night custom is to hide an almond in rice pudding.

11

◄ Cooking salmon in the open air in Finland. Fish is a staple food of many northern European countries.

In England, roast beef with roast potatoes and Yorkshire pudding is a traditional Sunday dinner, although nowadays many people choose chicken, lamb, pork, or a vegetarian option instead. England is also known for its traditional cooked breakfast of bacon and eggs, which are fried with other foods such as tomatoes and sausages. The Scottish national dish is haggis (sheep's stomach stuffed with the minced heart and liver of a sheep or calf, with onions, oatmeal, and seasonings). Served each year on January 25 to celebrate the birth of the Scottish poet Robert Burns, it is carried into the gathering by the chef, behind the bagpiper in full highland dress.

Pizza was originally the breakfast food of the ancient Romans. The people of Naples invented Neapolitan pizza, using local cheese and tomatoes. Another Italian dish is pasta, which was probably brought to Italy by Arab invaders, although one tradition says that the explorer Marco Polo introduced it from China in the 13th century. There are hundreds of types of pasta in Italy, and each region has its own traditional dish, such as the hot pepper pasta eaten in the south, or sweet pasta made with cinnamon and sugar which is eaten in Venice.

Each European country has its own traditional foods and recipes. The herring is one of Europe's oldest foods. In Viking times (8th-11th centuries A.D.), smoked and salted herring was a valuable winter food, since they could be stored easily. Today, they are very popular in Scandinavian countries where they are eaten in Danish open sandwiches and other cold meals. Germany is famous for its sausages and cold meats. A traditional German dish is Heaven and Earth, which contains sausages cooked with potatoes (that grow into the earth) and apples (that grow toward the sky).

◀ Paella, the traditional rice and seafood dish of Spain.

Bread sculpted into decorative shapes on sale at a market on the Greek island of Crete. Decorative foods are eaten at holidays all over Europe. ▼

Harvest celebrations are traditional in many European countries. People take fruit, vegetables, and flowers to harvest festivals in churches and schools and sing harvest hymns. A loaf of bread shaped like a sheaf of wheat is often the centerpiece of the ceremony. Bread has always been important in the European diet. It is also the ritual food of the Christian religion, representing the body of Christ in church services. Cakes are often baked to celebrate important events in life, such as weddings, christenings, and birthdays.

▲ **Two Spanish women preparing the spice saffron. Saffron comes from crocus flowers and features in many traditional dishes both in Spain and worldwide.**

In Greece and the Balkans, the tradition of cooking kebabs, or food on skewers, is said to have originated from Turkish soldiers spearing pieces of lamb on their swords and roasting them over an open fire. In Spain, the national dish of paella, made from rice, seafood and saffron, was created in Valencia and originally contained frogs, snails, eels, and green beans. Frogs' legs and snails are both delicacies in France. The ancient Gauls once enjoyed snails as a dessert and the Romans had snaileries where the snails were fattened on wine and bran. Frogs' legs were popular in the Middle Ages, especially during Lent.

Today, they are eaten mainly in France, Germany, and Italy, usually fried in butter and served with a sauce. They taste like tender chicken.

European feasts often include roast meat. Most elaborate is the traditional Sardinian feast of calves stuffed with smaller animals such as goats, pigs, and hares, roasted over an open fire. In Scandinavian countries, a popular feast is the smörgasbord, a table with lots of different hot and cold dishes laid out together, according to an ancient Norse custom. Russian feasts have several courses, with snacks such as smoked fish and caviar eaten between each course. New Year is a time for feasting all over Europe. Spaniards have a tradition of eating twelve grapes at New Year, one on each stroke of midnight, to bring good luck.

Make decorated Easter eggs

At Easter, Russian children decorate hard-boiled eggs. Although you can buy egg dyes or use food coloring, you can make your own using the juice from cooked spinach, beets, and even onion skins.

You will need:
1 lb. spinach or onion skins (for beets, use the red juice from the container)
2 eggs
vinegar or lemon juice
toothpicks

Ask an adult to help when using the stove.
1. Cook the spinach or onion skins in about 2 cups of water until the liquid has turned a deep color.

▲ Decorated eggs are symbolic of the new life of Easter and the spring.

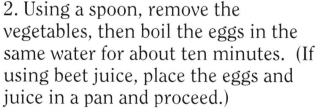

2. Using a spoon, remove the vegetables, then boil the eggs in the same water for about ten minutes. (If using beet juice, place the eggs and juice in a pan and proceed.)

3. Remove the eggs from the water and let them cool.

4. Dip a toothpick in vinegar and scratch a pattern onto the dyed eggs.

15

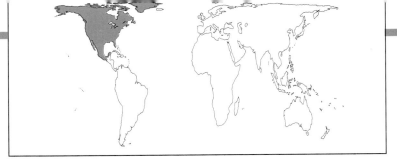

North America

Food traditions in North America combine many influences, including those of Native Americans and the early settlers. Native Americans were skilled at growing corn, beans, and potatoes, including sweet potatoes. They also tapped maple trees to collect sap to make syrup. From corn they created corn pudding, popcorn, hominy grits, and succotash, which is made of corn and lima beans. A dish of white beans slowly cooked with maple sugar and bear fat was adapted by the settlers, who used beans, pork, onions, and molasses to make the now famous Boston baked beans. Pumpkins became the main dessert ingredient in a favorite dessert pie. Another specialty from the early years of North American history is the New England clambake, a shellfish extravaganza consisting of lobsters, clams, oysters, and other food cooked between layers of seaweed in a rocky pit.

Harvested pumpkins in California. ▶

Main picture: Fish being dried in the open air in Greenland.

Corn on the cob being roasted at a stall in Mexico City. Corn is grown and used in traditional dishes throughout Mexico. ▶

Every year, on the fourth Thursday in November in the United States and the second Monday in October in Canada, people celebrate the feast of Thanksgiving. This feast dates back to the time of the Pilgrim Fathers, who traveled from Great Britain in the *Mayflower* in 1620, to escape religious persecution. Life was hard for the settlers, and many died before the first harvest was successfully gathered in. In the fall of 1621, at Plymouth, Massachusetts, the survivors held a great outdoor feast to give thanks for the harvest. Native Americans brought deer and wild turkeys, and the settlers snared geese, ducks, and fish and gathered plums, grapes, and watercress for the feast. Later, as more settlers arrived, the custom spread. Today, Thanksgiving is a national holiday and is celebrated as a happy family occasion. People feast on roast turkey stuffed with cornbread and served with cranberries, followed by pumpkin pie.

Mexican cooking reflects the influence of both the indigenous peoples, such as the Maya and Aztecs, and the Spanish and French settlers of the 15th and 16th centuries. The people who live in the Yucatán of southern Mexico are descendants of the Maya. They still use a traditional *pibil* method of cooking dishes by steaming meat wrapped in banana leaves over a pit in the ground filled with red-hot stones. In the north, a traditional method of preserving beef by drying is still practiced. The beef, called *cecina*, is sprinkled with salt and allowed to dry in the sun, then it is rubbed with lemon juice and pepper and left for two more days. It is made tender by pounding before being folded and finally stored.

A Huichol woman drying corn, an ▶
important crop that
the Huichol celebrate.

◀ **A woman making tortillas in Mexico**.

Throughout Mexico, corn, beans, and chili peppers are used in traditional dishes. Corn is used to make flat pancakes called tortillas and in soups, stews, and drinks. The Huichol people of southwest Mexico hold special festivals at corn planting and corn harvesting time. They paint their faces with a yellow dye made from the *uxa* plant, and they sing, dance, and feast on foods and drinks made from corn.

Fiestas, or festivals, are an important part of Mexican culture. On November 2 every year, Mexican people celebrate the Day of the Dead when they remember their dead loved ones. They carry candles, flowers, and food to their graves, and lots of toys and sweets celebrating death are sold at stalls. There are candy-sugar skulls, skeletons, and coffins, and pan de muertos (bread of the dead), which is bread that has been baked in the shape of a bone.

A popular Mexican dish for special occasions is *mole poblano*, which dates back to pre-Columbian times. This is turkey cooked in a sauce that contains 29 ingredients, including chili and chocolate.

A form of Mexican ▶ *pan de muertos* (bread of the dead), on sale during celebrations for the Day of the Dead (November 2).

Central and South America

Native peoples, African slaves, and European settlers, especially the Spanish and Portuguese, have all contributed to the food traditions of Central and South America. Corn, beans, potatoes, and rice are the staple crops of the area and are included in many traditional dishes. Some regional foods still use the ingredients of native cooking, such as roast peccary (a kind of wild pig), armadillo, alligator, iguana eggs and meat, and a type of large ant. Traditional methods of cooking also survive, such as the *pachamanca* used in Peru. This is an oven dug out of the earth to cook pork, goat, or chicken with corn, potatoes, and herbs. In Brazil, native peoples use cassava flour, cocoa, sweet potatoes, and peanuts. African people, brought to the region as slaves in the 17th century, introduced yams, coconuts, and the palm oil that is widely used for frying. In Ecuador, it is a tradition on the feast of All Saints to make hundreds of decorated sugar cakes that families eat near the graves of their dead loved ones.

▲ Hot potato pancakes on sale at a market in Ecuador.

Main picture: A colorful food market in a village square in Peru.

Inset: Corn features in many Central and South American dishes. These Chipaya women in Peru are sifting grain, preparing it for storage.

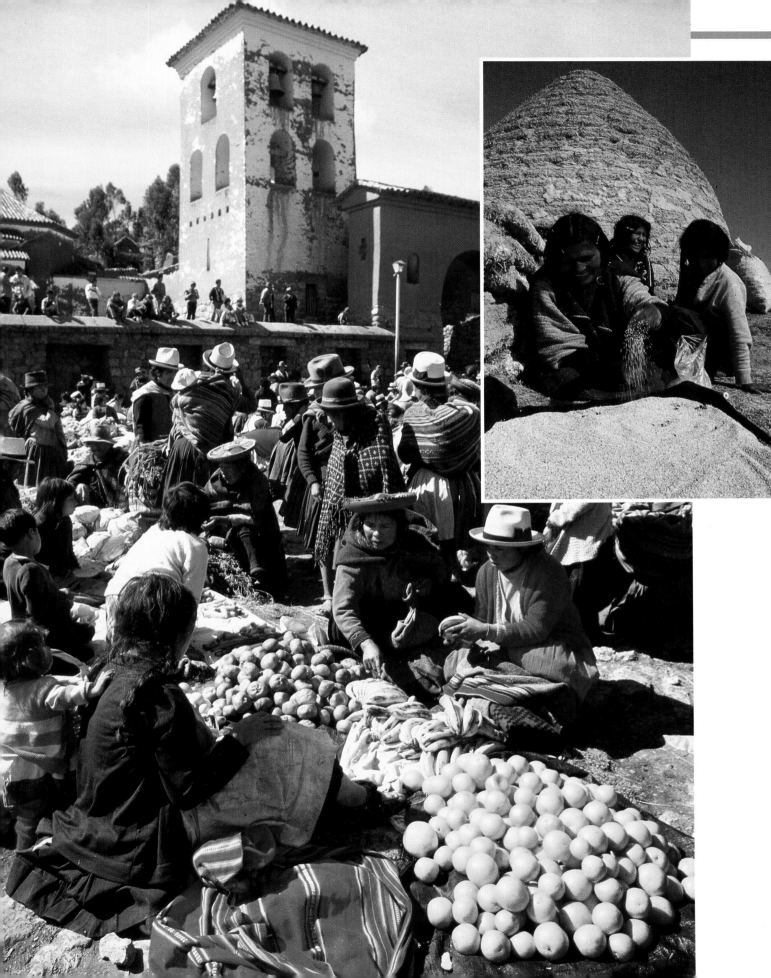

◀ The peoples of the Xingu Basin of the Amazon River, like the Arara, are hunter gatherers. Monkeys caught in the forest provide them with meat.

▲ The sugarcane harvest is always celebrated with a carnival in Barbados, in the Caribbean.

The food traditions of the Caribbean islands are a mixture created by the Arawak and Carib peoples and by settlers of many nationalities: Dutch, French, Spanish, British, Asian, and African. Rice and beans, a favorite dish with local variations on many of the islands, is actually made from rice and beans and has its origins in the bean dishes of Africa. Jerk Pork, a Jamaican dish of seasoned and spiced pork, dates back to an Arawak method of cooking pork. *Eskovitch*, a traditional dish of marinated fish, was introduced by Spanish settlers in the 17th century, while Dutch settlers created a recipe of shrimp-filled Edam cheeses. Each island has its own cooking methods, which include stewing, frying, and pot roasting in Dutch ovens (shallow, flat-bottomed pans) or cooking on flat iron griddles called *tawa*, which were introduced by Asian immigrants in the 19th century.

▲ Akee, a tropical fruit that is used in many traditional Jamaican dishes.

Jamaican Rice and Beans (serves 4)

Each island has its own recipe for rice and beans so the flavor varies from island to island. The recipe below is Jamaican. You could also add 3-4 strips of chopped, cooked bacon, as people do in Guadeloupe.

You will need:
2 tbsp. vegetable oil
1 medium-sized onion
1 clove garlic, finely chopped
2 cups long-grain rice
2 15 oz. cans coconut milk or 1 pkg. dried coconut and 4 cups water
a sprig of fresh thyme or 1/2 tsp. dried thyme
1/2 tsp. salt
2 16 oz. cans red kidney beans, drained. (You may use black-eyed peas or other beans if you prefer.)

You will use the stove to prepare this dish. Please ask an adult to help you with this recipe and any time you use the stove.

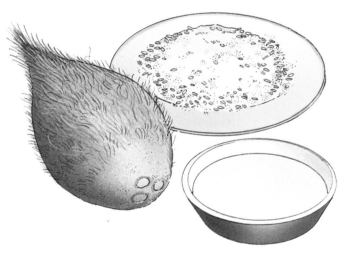

1. Rinse and drain the beans with a sieve. Set beans aside in a bowl.

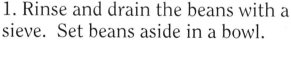

2. If you are using dried coconut you will have to make coconut "milk." Heat 4 cups of water in a saucepan and remove from heat. Stirring occasionally, soak dried coconut in the hot water for 15 minutes. Strain the mixture with the sieve, saving the liquid in a bowl. Use the back of a serving spoon to squeeze all of the liquid from the coconut.

You can check from time to time to see if any more water is needed to help the rice cook. It should be fluffy, not dry or soggy, when it is ready. Serve the rice and beans hot.

3. Heat the oil in a medium saucepan and gently fry the onion and garlic until just tender.

4. Add the rice, coconut milk, thyme, and salt to the pan. Slowly bring to a boil then lower the heat, cover, and simmer gently until all the coconut milk is absorbed and the rice is tender.

5. Add the beans and heat for a few minutes. Serve at once.

Africa

Africa is a vast continent that is inhabited by many different peoples with their own cultures, religions, languages, and food traditions. Differences in land, climate, and lifestyle mean that the foods eaten and the way they are prepared vary among regions and peoples. In western Africa more fish is eaten than meat. Because much of the population is Muslim, laws of the Koran regarding food, such as a law that forbids eating pork, are obeyed. In eastern Africa more meat is eaten, but meat is generally expensive to produce, so only small amounts are used to flavor rice and vegetable dishes. Chicken is often cooked for special occasions. *Jollof* rice, a traditional west African recipe, uses chicken or beef in a dish of rice and vegetables, flavored with peppers and spices. In north African cooking, fresh and dried fruits are often used to sweeten various dishes. South of the Sahara desert, however, using fruit would be against the traditional taboos of certain peoples, which prevent men from eating sweet foods they consider feminine. In this southern region, many dishes combine meat, fish, and vegetables in soups and stews.

Pigs' feet and heads on sale at a market in Cairo, Egypt. ▶

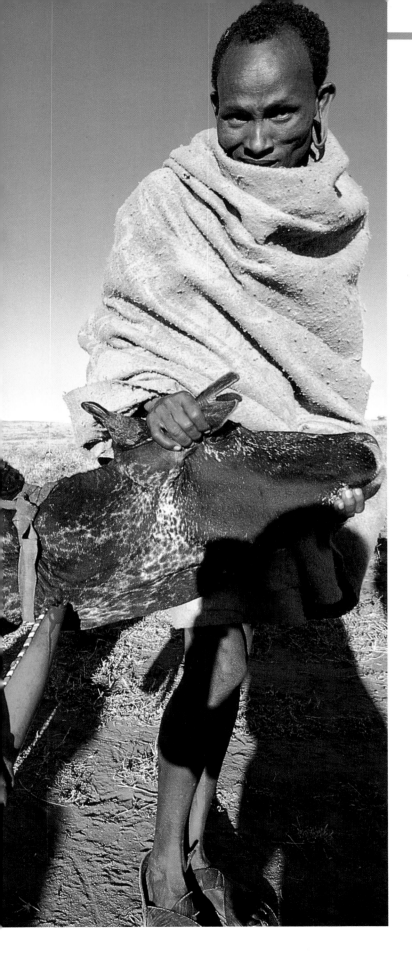

For centuries, Africa has traded with and been explored by peoples from the Middle East, China, India, and Europe, and their influence has contributed to African food traditions. Preserving meat or fish by salting may have originated from the Arab camel caravans that once traveled down from the north. In Angola, one traditional dish uses flaked, salted fish cooked in a large pot with potatoes, green peppers, and onions and is served with boiled eggs and olives.

Couscous, the national dish of Morocco, is thought to have originated with the Berber people. Each region has developed its own variation of couscous, a form of semolina that is cooked by steaming. Flavorings range from nuts and fruits to elaborate meat and vegetable creations.

In other parts of Africa, nomadic peoples like the pygmies of the Congo Basin hunt animals and gather fruit, nuts, and plants to eat. In the grasslands of Kenya, the Masai depend in part on the milk and blood of their cattle herds. Masai animals are killed only when they are old or for ceremonial purposes such as a boy's initiation into manhood, when he drinks the blood of a bullock before eating a meal of meat and milk. The Kikuyu of Kenya celebrate special occasions with barbecues of *mahu* (sheep's liver) and *mara* (cow's liver), stuffed with onions and animal blood.

◄ **Masai herdsmen taking blood from a cow. Cattle's blood is an important part of the Masai diet.**

▲ **Preparing food for a religious festival in Morocco**.

There are many African festivals and rituals surrounding the planting and harvesting of crops. Staple crops include corn, cassava, plantain, beans and okra. Festivals of thanks are held for a good harvest, and some cultures present the first fruits of the harvest to their gods or to the spirits of their ancestors. It is traditional to eat the remains of the previous year's harvest before tasting the new crop. The Dogon people of west Africa celebrate each new crop by dancing and wearing traditional masks. The people of Argungu in Nigeria hold a fishing festival in February, when they compete to see who can catch the most fish.

Christians sometimes set aside a plot of land in their community that they call God's acre. On this land they

This woman in Zambia is pouring beans ▶ from a calabash, a hollowed-out gourd used for storing food.

▲ **A woman selling cassava, a staple African crop**.

grow crops to be sold at harvest festivals to raise funds for their church or other local causes. Christians may celebrate Easter and Christmas with the roast meat and vegetables traditionally eaten in Europe, but there are also local festive dishes such as *yassa* from Senegal. This is made from chicken marinated in garlic, cloves, and other spices, then fried and served with rice. Traditionally, family members or friends gather in a circle and eat with their fingers from a large, common plate.

◀ **A spice stall in Madagascar. Spices are used in recipes all over Africa and around the world**.

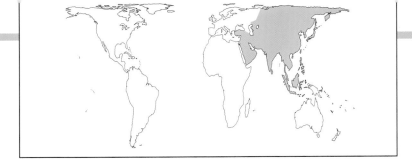

Asia

China is a very large country with a vast population made up of over 50 ethnic groups, each with its own customs and food traditions. Food markets in China are colorful places with hundreds of different foods on sale, including snakes, locusts, chickens, and ducks' feet. There is also a strong vegetarian tradition, encouraged by religions like Buddhism and Taoism that believe all living things are sacred.

Many recipes, cooking techniques, and utensils that originated in ancient China are still used today. About 5,000 years ago, the Chinese invented the wok, an iron pot with a curved shape that cooks food quickly by steaming or stir-frying. The wok keeps food fresh and crunchy and saves fuel. In China, chopsticks have been used for eating since about 1600 BC.

◄ Woks are used for cooking many foods in China.

▲ Sheep being dried for storage on a balcony in Mongolia.

▲ This Chinese candymaker is creating a decorative candy from fine strands of sugar.

The Chinese believe that everything you eat affects the body's balance and energies, which they call *qi*. Everyone must try to balance hot foods (such as meat and spicy dishes) with cold foods (such as citrus fruits and vegetables). A traditional greeting in China is to say "Have you eaten?" If you have, all is well. Food is often taken as a gift when visiting friends or relatives. Some foods are believed to bring good luck: noodles represent long life and are often given at birthdays; cake is a symbol of success.

Festival days have special food traditions. The Chinese moon festival, which celebrates an ancient legend, is held in the fall at the time of the full moon. The legend is about a wicked emperor who was given a magic potion that would let him live forever. To save the people, his wife drank the potion. The emperor was furious and tried to kill her, but the gods lifted her up and took her to the moon where she lives today.

During the festival, people carry colorful lanterns shaped like animals or fish. They eat moon cakes – round pastries filled with red bean and lotus-seed paste – and moon-shaped fruits such as peaches, melons, and apples.

The Dragon Boat Festival is held on the fifth day of the fifth month in the Chinese year, usually in early June. Boats shaped like dragons are raced in memory of the third-century poet Qu Yuan, who drowned himself in a lake. Legend has it that the villagers threw rice dumplings into the water to stop his body from being eaten by dragons. At the festival, people eat *zong-zi* – parcels of rice and sweet or flavorful ingredients wrapped in lotus leaves.

Chinese New Year, which is held in the spring, is a time for feasting. In the north, families join together to make dumplings filled with ground meat called *jiao-zi*. A New Year's cake, *niangao*, is made from brown sugar and rice, and *tang yuan* – little red and white balls of rice flour, sometimes with a sesame filling – are also popular.

Japan shares some food traditions with China, including the customs of sitting on the floor at a low table to eat, using chopsticks, and serving all the dishes together for guests to help themselves. As in China, there are many traditional dishes based on rice, noodles, and soya beans. Rice is the staple crop of Japan and is eaten with every meal. It is the ritual food of the ancient Shinto religion, and rice grains are traditionally thrown at Japanese weddings to bring fertility to the newly married couple. In the spring, there is a special ceremony in which the emperor plants the first new rice. In the fall the people celebrate the rice harvest with the New Taste festival, now called Labor Thanksgiving Day. Everyone sits down to a good feast of the new rice crop, accompanied with rice wine.

Fish is also important in traditional Japanese cooking and may be salted or dried, grilled, boiled, or eaten raw. It takes several years for a Japanese cook to learn how to prepare raw fish delicacies such as sushi and sashimi.

Japanese New Year is celebrated with foods in the lucky colors of red and white. Red and white fish are mixed together in fish cakes, white turnip is wrapped around red salmon, and rice is colored red with aduki beans in the popular dish of seki-han. At midnight on New Year's Eve, Japanese families eat bowls of hot noodles. In the morning, everyone dresses in traditional kimonos and breakfasts on *ozoni*, a thick vegetable soup, with rice cakes. Then comes the lunchtime feast, which is set out in lacquered boxes containing fish, vegetables, soy beans, and rolls of seaweed stuffed with herring. A favorite dessert is *kuri kinton*, which is made from chestnuts, sweet potatoes, and sugar. Tangerines, which are symbolic of the sun, may be given as New Year gifts to bring good luck.

The presentation of food in Japan is very important. Skilled cooks try to create a beautiful picture of food on a plate, sometimes decorating it with fruits and vegetables that are carved to look like flowers.

▲ This vendor in Japan is dressed as one of the Japanese gods of fortune for the New Year festival. He is selling foods in lucky New Year colors.

The Iban people of Borneo in Southeast Asia worship a rice spirit. They hold ceremonies at planting and harvest time, celebrating with several days and nights of feasting and dancing. In parts of Indonesia, it is traditional when eating rice to leave a spoonful for the rice goddess, unlike in Japan, where leaving rice is bad manners. Many other food traditions in Southeast Asia are connected with religion. Buddhists in countries such as Thailand still practice the ancient tradition of taking offerings of food to the monks every day.

How to use chopsticks

Chopsticks are used for eating in China, Japan, and parts of Southeast Asia. For family meals, everyone has his or her own rice bowl and uses chopsticks to pick from other dishes on the table. Even small children are skilled at using chopsticks, although they may lift their bowls to make it easier.

1. Take hold of the thick end of one of your chopsticks and rest it between your thumb and index finger and on the center of your middle finger. This chopstick should not move.

2. Slide the second chopstick between your index finger and thumb, holding it like a pencil so that the tips of your chopsticks pinch together then pull apart. You may need to practice for a while before you can start picking up pieces of food.

Never cross your chopsticks when laying them down. In China this is believed to bring bad luck.

▲ **These women are using chopsticks to eat noodles.**

Each region in the subcontinent of India has its own traditional dishes. Kashmir is famous for meat and chickpeas; Madras for vegetarian dishes made from tamarind, semolina and coconut; Bengal for sweet desserts and fish; and Delhi for tandoori cooking. The tandoor, a clay oven, is widely used in northern India and Pakistan. Meat is marinated in yogurt and spices, then cooked quickly over charcoal in the tandoor. Spices are very important in Indian cooking; as many as twelve spices may be used in one dish. There is no Indian word for curry (*kari* means sauce). Each dish has its own name, according to the different ingredients and spices used.

More than half the people in India are vegetarian, some for religious reasons and others because they cannot afford meat or fish. Their diet is based on grains, lentils, vegetables, and rice. Many Hindus and some Sikhs are vegetarians because they believe that it is wrong to kill animals. The preparation and serving of food is an important part of the Hindu, Sikh, and Muslim religions. After a religious service, Sikhs share food that has been blessed to symbolize their strength as a community. Hindus also bless food before eating, offering part of it to their gods. At festivals, special sweet dishes, such as halva, which is semolina rice heated with ghee then cooked in milk with cardamom seeds, are prepared as offerings.

Sweets for festivals may be decorated with finely beaten silver and gold.

Indian weddings, whether Hindu, Muslim, Sikh, or Christian, are celebrated with special foods. The sweet dishes may include *jilebees* (semolina fried in ghee and dipped in a saffron-flavored syrup), *shrikhand* (a kind of spiced yogurt), and *ladoos* (balls of semolina and sugar). At Hindu wedding ceremonies, the bride and groom stand in a shallow basket while rice is poured over their heads to bless their marriage.

Traditionally in India, food is eaten with the right hand. In the south, it may be served on banana leaves. In central India, small helpings of each dish are placed on a *thali*, or tray.

The Middle East

▲ **Traditional Middle Eastern bread, coated with sesame seeds.**

Many food traditions in the Middle East have ancient origins dating back to early Bedouin and peasant cooking. *Molokhia*, a green, spinach-like soup, was first made in ancient Egypt. One of the oldest sweetmeats, *Faludhaj*, a Persian recipe of marzipan with rosewater-flavored dough, may originally have been made for pilgrims traveling to Mecca in Saudi Arabia, the birthplace of the prophet Muhammad. Other recipes have survived unchanged for hundreds of years, passed down from generation to generation. Stewed lamb with yogurt served on a bed of rice dates back to ancient Bedouin life in Jordan and Syria.

Some foods have religious traditions surrounding them. Eating honey and syrups is believed to make life sweeter and to keep away the *djinn* (devil). Garlic is thought to protect against evil. The Koran, the Muslim holy book, contains laws about food, such as forbidding pork and fasting at certain times. Fasting is believed to cleanse the mind and body. Once a year, in the ninth month of their calendar, Muslims celebrate Ramadan, eating nothing between dawn and dusk for a month. At the end of Ramadan is the feast of *Eid al Fitr*. Traditional festive dishes include stuffed lamb or chicken served with rice and salads, followed by special desserts and sweetmeats.

Another ancient festival is *Now Ruz*, the Iranian New Year, which is celebrated on March 21, the first day of spring. About ten days earlier new grain is sown, and on the eve of *Now Ruz* the fresh shoots are picked and divided among the family. Tied with ribbons, each bunch of shoots is placed on a special table called a *haftsin,* with other foods that symbolize the roots of life, such as apples, herbs, garlic, and vinegar. On the 13th day of *Now Ruz*, Iranian families go for a picnic. They tie the new shoots to the front of the car and somewhere on their journey they throw them into a river or stream.

Over many generations, the Jewish people have traveled throughout the world, and their history is reflected in their food laws, called *kashrut*. Practicing Jews should eat kosher food, which is food allowed by these laws. Certain foods are forbidden, such as pork, game, and shellfish. Meat and dairy products must never be cooked or eaten together, so in kosher kitchens there are two sets of cooking utensils.

On Friday evenings, the beginning of the Jewish Sabbath, families light candles, say prayers, and eat a special meal together. Two braided loaves of bread, called challah, are blessed and eaten, symbolizing the double portion of food that their god is believed to have given to the Jews when they were wandering in the desert after escaping slavery in Egypt. Fish cakes, prepared with onions, eggs, and matzoh meal, and chicken are also traditional foods for the Sabbath.

At *Rosh Hashanah*, the Jewish New Year, Jewish people eat sweet foods such as honeycake and bread and apples dipped in honey, to bring a sweet year. *Yom Kippur*, nine days later, is an important day of fasting. The festival of Passover (*Pesach*), in early spring, celebrates the time when Jewish people escaped from slavery in Egypt. They were in such a hurry that they could not wait for their newly made bread to rise, so at Passover only unleavened bread is eaten. People also eat other symbolic foods, such as salt to represent the tears their ancestors cried as slaves, eggs and scallions for new life, and *charoseth*, a sweet paste of fruit and nuts, which represents the sweetness of freedom.

The festival of *Shavuot* celebrates the giving of the Law to the prophet Moses on Mount Sinai in Egypt, as told in the Bible. It is said that the Jews waited so long for Moses to return that their milk turned into cheese, so traditional foods eaten at Shavuot include cheesecake and cheese-filled pancakes.

Another festival, Chanukah, celebrates the miracle of the oil, when one day's supply of oil for the holy lamp in the temple at Jerusalem lasted eight days. At Chanukah, foods cooked in oil, such as latkes (potato pancakes) and doughnuts are eaten.

A Jewish family celebrating the festival ▶ of Passover with the traditional meal.

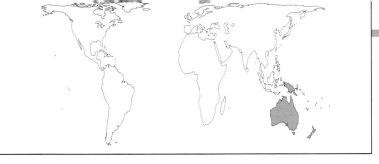

The Pacific

Hunting and gathering food is an age-old tradition for the indigenous peoples of the Pacific region. The Aborigines of Australia are skilled at hunting with boomerangs, spears, digging sticks, traps, and nets. These have been used to catch every kind of "bush tucker" (food), from kangaroos (now a protected species) and emus, to snakes, lizards, birds, and bats. Women gather yams, berries, grubs, worms, birds' eggs, and wild honey. They make bush bread, called damper, by grinding grass seeds on flat stones to make a simple dough. In Arnhem Land, northern Australia, another traditional source of food for the Aborigines is water-lily bulbs, which they dig from riverbeds with their feet and either cook over a fire or pound into dough.

Seafood and ▶ freshwater fish, such as these *yabbies* (crayfish), are very popular all over the Pacific region.

Main picture: Kangaroo tail is a traditional delicacy for the Aborigines of Western Australia.

40

The honey-ant, which has an abdomen containing a sack of honey, is a unique delicacy for the Papunya of Central Australia. Aboriginal food consumption varies. Foods taboo or sacred to one group may have the opposite meaning for another, depending on local folklore or mythology. One group that lives on the New South Wales coast, for example, cannot eat the goanna (a kind of lizard) because it is special to their particular mythology.

Traditional Aboriginal corroborees, or gatherings, are often seasonal events, based on food sources. One of the strangest in Aboriginal history was the Great Moth Feast at the Bogong Mountains near Canberra, when hundreds of Aborigines of different clans would gather together to eat the large-winged moths that collected in the caves.

Traditionally, meat was cooked in underground pits or over a fire. The Maori, who settled in New Zealand from Polynesia hundreds of years ago, steamed food in underground ovens called *hangi*, and this method is still used in New Zealand when entertaining large groups of people. The Maori cooked foods like fish and sweet potatoes by wrapping them in leaves and steaming them over hot stones. Australians and New Zealanders today continue this ancient tradition by having barbecues, which are popular everywhere both for special occasions and for family meals.

◀ **This Maori woman is using a traditional method of cooking in naturally occurring thermal (hot) water in New Zealand**.

▲ **An Aboriginal woman digging for honey-ants**.

Some traditional Australian dishes date back to the arrival of the early pioneers and settlers from Europe. These include shearer's stew, made of lamb and vegetables eaten with dumplings; parakeet pie, which is made from small parrots; beef and hard-boiled eggs cooked in pastry; and kangaroo-tail soup. The settlers also brought their own food traditions with them. At Christmas, some Australian families eat the European-style feast of roast turkey and plum pudding, even though it is midsummer and very hot. Harvest is also celebrated as in Europe, although in Australia it takes place in March. Gifts of fruit, vegetables, preserved foods, and flowers are taken to churches, and people sing traditional hymns of thanksgiving.

Ethnic communities celebrate their own festivals with feasting. Every year, the Caldoche people of New Caledonia, New Zealand, who are of French origin, have a special outdoor lunch or picnic to celebrate Bastille Day.

43

Some indigenous peoples hold traditional feasts to celebrate their staple crops or livestock. For the peoples of Papua New Guinea, the Pig Festival is the most important social, religious, and festive time of the year. The Wahgi people paint their faces and bodies and wear elaborate decorations, such as feathered headdresses, for the ceremony. Hundreds of pigs, the traditional symbol of wealth for the Wahgi, are sacrificed to please the ghosts of their ancestors, and there is feasting, singing, and dancing. On the Trobriand Islands, where the yam is the staple food, the yam harvest is met with weeks of

celebrating. Women from each village decorate their bodies and carry their yams to a gathering place to be judged for the prize of "good gardener."

These many traditions around the world show that food is not just a means of staying alive but is an important part of social, cultural, and religious life. It may be part of the religious practice of a society, and it often carries its own mythology and symbolism. In the lives of individuals, food can be used to mark important events such as birth, coming of age, marriage, and death. Like literature, art, music and costume, food reflects the beliefs, ideas, and histories of people around the world.

Roast suckling pig is the traditional festive food of the peoples of the Pacific islands, where pigs have been a symbol of wealth for hundreds of years. ▼

Glossary

Aduki bean A small red bean, popular in Japanese cooking, thought to bring luck.

Cassava A vegetable with an edible root.

Caviar The salted roe (eggs) of the sturgeon fish.

Charcoal Wood burned in a special way, used for cooking and drawing.

Chili A hot spice from a red or green fruit, often called hot pepper.

Citrus fruits A family of fruits including lemons, oranges, limes and grapefruit.

Delicacy Special, highly prized food.

Ethnic Belonging to a group of people with a common cultural background.

Fasting Going without food.

Folklore The traditional myths and beliefs of a people.

Ghee Clarified butter. Made by heating butter and skimming off the top layer. Ghee is used in a lot of Indian cooking.

Herring A type of fish found in the North Atlantic.

Iguana A large lizard.

Immigrants People who have moved into a country from elsewhere.

Indigenous Native, or coming from a particular part of the world.

Initiation Going through a special ritual in order to become a full or adult member of a society or group.

Kimono A long, loose Japanese robe.

Lotus A kind of plant. Lotus-seeds are sweet and used in Chinese cooking.

Marinade/marinate A method of preparing meat, fish, or vegetables with spices, sauces, or juices in order to give them flavor and make them tender.

Marzipan A paste of ground almonds and sugar.

Matzoh Bread made without a raising agent such as yeast.

Mythology Stories and beliefs about the origins of the world and the forces that made it.

Nomadic The way of life of peoples who travel in order to find water and food for themselves and their animals.

Noodles Strips of dough made from flour and eggs.

Norse Ancient Scandinavian.

Okra A kind of vegetable often used in African and southern cooking.

Plantain A fruit from a tropical plant similar to a banana. Used in the cuisine of Africa and the Caribbean.

Polo, Marco A famous merchant and explorer (1254-1324) who traveled from Europe to Asia.

Pre-Columbian Refers to time before Christopher Columbus arrived in America.

Ritual A service or gathering connected with religious or other traditional beliefs.

Staple foods/crops Foods that grow well in an area and provide a basic element in the diet of that area.

Superstitious Believing in the supernatural.

Sweetmeats Treats, usually made with sugar or chocolate.

Symbolic/symbolize Something which represents something else.

Taboo Something banned or forbidden.

Torah Laws of the Jewish faith.
Tamarind A kind of tangy tropical fruit.
Unleavened Made without yeast or any other kind of rising substance.

Books to read

Food Around the World. A series of ten books on food by country.
New York: Thomson Learning, published from 1993-1995.

Dando, William and Dando, Caroline Z. *A Reference Guide To World Hunger.* Hillside, NJ: Enslow Publishers, 1991.

Perl, Lila. *Slumps, Grunts, and Snickerdoodles: What Colonial America Ate & Why.* New York: Clarion Books, 1979.

Tesar, Jenny. *Food & Water: Threats, Shortages & Solutions.* Vero Beach, FL: Rourke, 1992.

Information about individual cultures may also be found in the 48-volume Cultures of the World series by Marshall Cavendish Corporation (North Bellmore, NY), or in your library's encyclopedia.

Index

The foods and recipes in this book come from many different cultures. Various types of food are listed in the index, such as "vegetables," "meat," and "staple crops." If you want to see how different foods are used, look at entries such as "festivals," "feasts," and "religions." You can use the "peoples" entry to look up foods and eating customs from the cultures mentioned in the book.

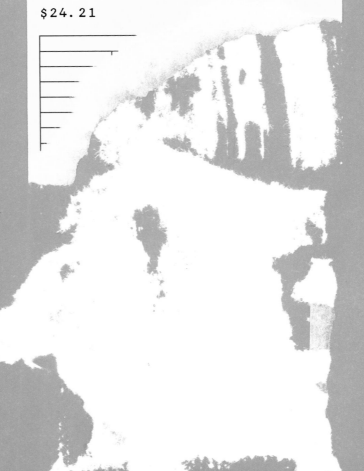